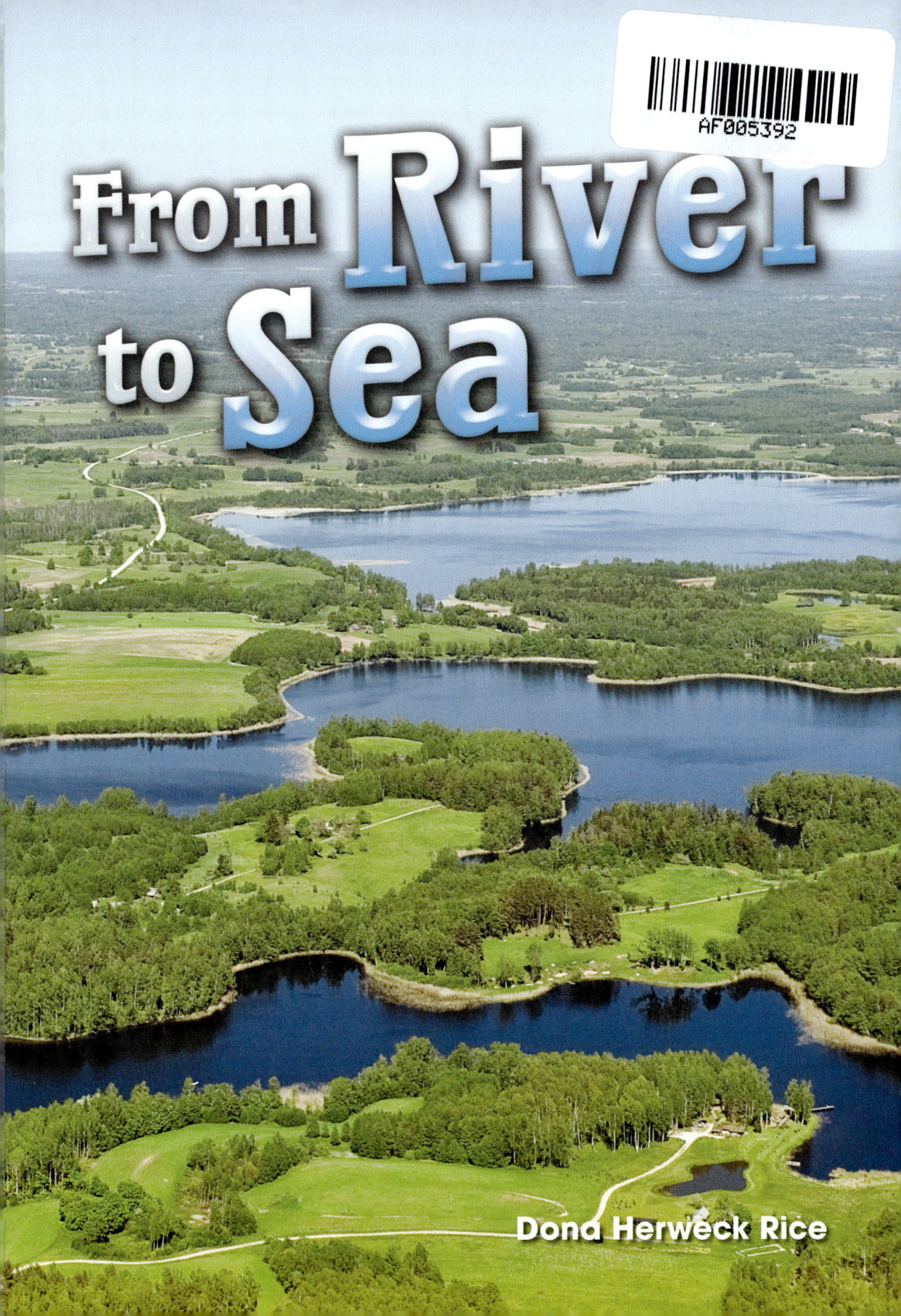

From River to Sea

Dona Herweck Rice

Published by Pearson Education Limited, 80 Strand, London, WC2R 0RL.

www.pearsonschools.co.uk

First published as *Water Bodies* in 2015 by Teacher Created Materials. This edition is published as *River to Sea* by Pearson Education Limited by arrangement with Teacher Created Materials. All rights reserved.

© 2015 Teacher Created Materials, Inc.

Text by Dona Herweck Rice

22 21 20 19 18
10 9 8 7 6 5 4 3 2 1

British Library Cataloguing in Publication Data
A catalogue record for this book is available from the British Library

ISBN 978 0 435 19480 2

Copyright notice
All rights reserved. No part of this publication may be reproduced in any form or by any means (including photocopying or storing it in any medium by electronic means and whether or not transiently or incidentally to some other use of this publication) without the written permission of the copyright owner, except in accordance with the provisions of the Copyright, Designs and Patents Act 1988 or under the terms of a licence issued by the Copyright Licensing Agency, Barnards Inn, 86 Fetter Lane, London EC4A 1EN (www.cla.co.uk). Applications for the copyright owner's written permission should be addressed to the publisher.

Printed in China by Golden Cup

Acknowledgements
We would like to thank the following schools for their invaluable help in the development and trialling of the Bug Club resources: Bishop Road Primary School, Bristol; Blackhorse Primary School, Bristol; Hollingwood Primary School, West Yorkshire; Kingswood Parks Primary, Hull; Langdale CE Primary School, Ambleside; Pickering Infant School, Pickering; The Royal School, Wolverhampton; St Thomas More's Catholic Primary School, Hampshire; West Park Primary School, Wolverhampton.

The author and publisher would like to thank the following individuals and organisations for permission to reproduce photographs and illustrations:
Photographs
(Key: b-bottom; c-centre; l-left; r-right; t-top bck-background)
Cover Front: **Shutterstock:** Miks Mihails Ignats, Back: **Shutterstock** : Roberto Cerruti
Shutterstock: Miks Mihails Ignats 1, Roberto Cerruti 14b, Beth Swanson 3, Karel Bartik 4, Kataleewan intarachote 4-5bck, Aleksandar Todorovic 5, Frank L Junior 6-7bck, Sarah Cheriton-Jones 7t, Songquan Deng 7b, Makitalo 8-9bck, Catalin Petolea 8, Sannyday 9, Galyna Andrushko 10-11bck, Rich Carey 11b, Evgeny Sayfutdinov 12- 13bck, EastVillage Images 13, Yuriy Kulik 14-15bck, Boris Stroujko 15, Madlen 16, Md8speed 16bck, Ehrlif 17bck, Ivaschenko Roman 17, Straga 18, ESB Professional 20, Aphotostory 21, Mj - tim photography 24-25bck, Nicha 24, MarcelClemens 27b, Ivaschenko Roman 30b, Topseller 30-31t, Filip Fuxa 31b, Dudarev Mikhail 32, Baldyrgan . **123rf:** chr1 26-27bck .**NASA:** Nasa/Noaa Goes Project 10, 11t, 19, 23b, **Wikimedia Commons:** Sandister Tei 22-23t, **Getty Images:** Kali9/ iStock 6, Brian D Cruickshank/ Lonely Planet Images 22, Baldyrgan 10bl.
All illustrations: Teacher Created Materials(TCM).

Note from the publisher
Pearson has robust editorial processes, including answer and fact checks, to ensure the accuracy of the content in this publication, and every effort is made to ensure this publication is free of errors. We are, however, only human, and occasionally errors do occur. Pearson is not liable for any misunderstandings that arise as a result of errors in this publication, but it is our priority to ensure that the content is accurate. If you spot an error, please do contact us at resourcescorrections@pearson.com so we can make sure it is corrected.

Contents

A Watery Planet 4

Rivers, Lakes and Seas. 6

Water on Earth. 10

Man-made 20

The Wonder of Water 24

Let's Try It! 28

Glossary 30

Index 31

Your Turn! 32

A Watery Planet

You can splash in it, wash in it, swim in it or drink it – water is one of the most important things on Earth.

Rainbow trout live in fresh water.

We can't live without it, so it's a good thing that water is everywhere. Water covers much more than half of Earth. It's even found underground, in rivers and lakes.

This underground river is in the Philippines.

Rivers, Lakes and Seas

Nearly three-quarters of Earth's **surface** is covered in water. Sometimes the water stays in one place, like in a pond or lake. Sometimes it moves from place to place, like a river or a stream.

You are water!
Did you know that more than half of your body is made up of water?

a pond

River Thames, London, UK

Water collects in different parts of Earth's surface. It gathers in dips in the land, and flows into rivers. Water can fall as rain, hail or snow, or it can spring up from below the ground.

Because water is a liquid, it fills the shape of whatever holds it. Ponds and lakes can be any size and shape, depending on what the land underneath is like.

Capra Lake, Romania

evaporation from a river

Drip, drop, drip

The amount of water in lakes and rivers is always changing. **Precipitation**, such as rain, adds water to them. Lakes and rivers lose water through evaporation.

Water on Earth

You can find water all over Earth's surface, in lots of different forms. Some bodies of water are enormous, like oceans, and some are very small, like mountain streams. Some are always moving, and some are quite still.

Oceans

Almost all of Earth's water is in oceans. These huge areas of water cover most of the Earth. Oceans are made of salt water.

Lots of plants and animals live in oceans and seas, but there are big parts of the world's oceans that humans have never explored.

The Pacific Ocean is the largest ocean in the world.

Pacific Ocean

The Mediterranean Sea is almost completely surrounded by land.

Salty seas

Seas are like oceans, except they are blocked in by land on all or most sides.

Many lionfish live in the Pacific Ocean.

Lakes

Most lakes are made by nature, but some lakes are made by people. Whether they are natural or man-made, lakes are often beautiful places. People visit lakes to have fun doing water sports, fishing and watching out for wildlife.

Big lake

One-fifth of all fresh water on Earth is in Lake Baikal, one of Earth's deepest and largest lakes.

Lake Baikal is in Russia. The lake is 25 million years old!

Lakes are large areas of water that are mostly still. They are like basins in the ground. They are generally surrounded by land.

Although the water in a lake mostly stays still, rivers and streams often flow into and out of lakes.

Lake McDonald, in Montana, USA, has rivers that flow into it and rivers that flow out.

Ponds

A pond is a small area of water surrounded by land. It is not very deep and sunlight is able to reach the bottom. Many plants and animals live in ponds. You might see ducks and frogs in a pond. If you get your net out and go pond-dipping, you could find lots of water creatures, including water fleas, tadpoles and beetles.

Wood ducks live in ponds.

More than 1,000 types of animals live in ponds.

Puddles

A puddle is like a tiny pond, but it usually does not last long. It is small and easily dried by the sun's heat.

Wetlands

A wetland is land that is usually soaked with water. The water may not always be there – sometimes it dries up for a while, but it will always return. A wetland is filled with plant life. The plants that grow well there need very wet soil to survive.

Anything goes!

Water in a wetland can be fresh or salty. Swamps, marshes and bogs are types of wetlands.

Great willow-herbs are flowers that grow in wetlands.

Crayfish are animals that live in swamps.

Rivers

Rivers tend to flow towards a larger body of water – such as the sea or a lake. Some rivers end up underground. When the weather is hot and dry, some rivers dry up, but they come back when it rains again. Rivers can be any size – as wide as a field, or narrow enough to jump across.

Streams

Are streams and rivers different? Usually people think of streams as being smaller than rivers.

Rivers are usually fresh water.

Egypt

The Nile River is the longest river in Africa. It flows through nine countries. Egypt would be all desert if the Nile was not there. Very little rain falls in Egypt, but the Nile rises each year because of rains at its **source** in Ethiopia.

Man-made

Not every body of water is made by nature. People make or reshape some of them so that they can use them for travel, for example. People also make **dams** and reservoirs to control and store water.

The Grand Canal divides the city of Venice in Italy in two.

The Beijing-Hangzhou Grand Canal in China is the longest canal in the world.

Canals

Canals are like rivers, but they are made by people. People travel down canals in boats. Some canals were built to bring water to towns and villages. Sometimes people dig new canals where there aren't any rivers – and sometimes they make a canal by changing the way a river flows.

A girl carries water on her head after collecting it from Lake Volta.

Reservoirs

Reservoirs hold and store water. They can be natural or man-made. People sometimes build dams to control the water in a reservoir, so that there isn't too much or too little water. People need to be sure that they can get water from the reservoir when they need it.

Lake Volta is a reservoir in Ghana. It is the largest reservoir in the world.

Réservoir

The word *réservoir* is a French word meaning "storehouse".

The Wonder of Water

Water can create some amazing sights. Waterfalls happen when water from a river spills over the top of a cliff or a steep hillside. Angel Falls in Venezuela is the tallest waterfall in the world. It's nearly a kilometre high! Geysers are fantastic sights too. They happen when hot water from under the Earth gushes upwards.

a waterfall in southern Laos

Old Faithful, in Yellowstone National Park in the USA, is one of the most famous geysers in the world.

Old Faithful erupts every one to two hours.

Over time, oceans, rivers and lakes can change. Rivers and lakes get bigger or smaller when the weather changes.

Lake Tahoe in the USA

Even seas and oceans can change. If water levels rise, seas get bigger and cover more of the land. Long ago, a lot of the land that people live on now was under the sea. Maybe one day, far in the future, some of this land will be under the sea again.

These fossilised shells were discovered on land. This means that water used to cover that area.

Let's Try It!

Make your own rivers and lakes!

What you need

- clay
- sand
- tray
- water

What to do

1 Fill the tray with clay.

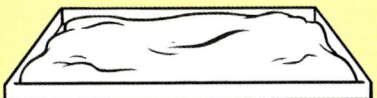

2 Mould the clay to make hills and valleys. Add sand to some areas of the clay.

3 Pour water over some of the clay and sand. Where does the water settle?

4 Gently tip and shake the tray. Add more water. What do you notice when you do these things?

Glossary

dams – barriers built across rivers to hold back water and form reservoirs

evaporation – process of changing from a liquid to a gas

precipitation – rain, snow and hail

source – place where something come from

surface – upper layer of an area of land or water

Index

bogs, 16

canals, 20, 22

dams, 20, 22

fresh water, 4, 12, 16, 18

lakes, 5, 6, 8, 9, 12, 13, 18, 22–23, 26, 32

marshes, 16

oceans, 10, 11, 26–27, 32

ponds, 7, 14–15

puddles, 7, 8, 14–15, 32

reservoirs, 20, 22–23

rivers, 5, 6–7, 9, 12, 13, 18–19, 21, 24

salt water, 10, 16

seas, 6, 7, 10–11, 18, 27

streams, 6, 10, 13, 18

swamps, 16, 17

waterfalls, 24, 31

wetlands, 16–17

Godafos Falls, Iceland

Your Turn!

Watching water

Visit a lake or river near your home. What do you see there? What do you hear and smell? Draw a picture of it, and write a sentence to describe it.